ADAPTED FOR SUCCESS

SNAKES
AND OTHER REPTILES

Andrew Solway

Heinemann
LIBRARY

www.heinemann.co.uk/library
Visit our website to find out more information about Heinemann Library books.

To order:
 Phone 44 (0) 1865 888066
 Send a fax to 44 (0) 1865 314091
Visit the Heinemann bookshop at www.heinemann.co.uk/library to browse our catalogue and order online.

First published in Great Britain by Heinemann Library, Halley Court, Jordan Hill, Oxford OX2 8EJ, part of Harcourt Education.
Heinemann is a registered trademark of Harcourt Education Ltd.

© Harcourt Education Ltd 2007
First published in paperback in 2008
The moral right of the proprietor has been asserted.

Editorial: Sarah Shannon and Lucy Beevor
Design: Richard Parker
Illustrations: Q2A Solutions
Picture Research: Mica Brancic and Susi Paz
Production: Chloe Bloom

Originated by Chroma Graphics (Overseas) Pte. Ltd.
Printed and bound in China by WKT Company Ltd.

10 digit ISBN 0 431 90667 X (hardback)
13 digit ISBN 978 0 431 90667 6
11 10 09 08 07
10 9 8 7 6 5 4 3 2 1

10 digit ISBN 0 431 90674 2 (paperback)
13 digit ISBN 978 0 431 90674 4
12 11 10 09 08
10 9 8 7 6 5 4 3 2 1

British Library Cataloguing in Publication Data
Solway, Andrew
Snakes and other reptiles. – (Adapted for success)
597.9'6
A full catalogue record for this book is available from the British Library.

Acknowledgements
The publishers would like to thank the following for permission to reproduce photographs:
Alamy p. 22 (David Hosking); Corbis pp. 31 (Australian Picture Library/Leo Meier), 24 (Chris Hellier), 12 (Frank Lane Picture Agency), 25 (Frank Lane Picture Agency/Ron Austing), 6 (Frans Lanting), 33 (Gallo Images/Rod Patterson), 10 (Gavriel Jecan), 27 (George McCarthy), 23 (Jim Zuckerman), 13 (Joe McDonald), 38 (Kelly-Mooney Photography), 39 (Ludovic Maisant), 37 (Martin Harvey), 9 (Steve Kaufman), 19 (Zefa/Kevin Schafer); Getty pp. 20 (Altrendo), 41 (Lonely Planet Images), 14, 21, 34, 35 (National Geographic), 5, 18 (Stone), 4, 26 (Taxi), 16 (The Image Bank); NHPA pp. 30 (Anthony Bannister), 8, 15, 29 (Daniel Heuclin), 40 (Joe Blossom); Science Photo Library pp. 32 (Alan Sirulnikoff), 43 (Bonnier Publications/Claus Lunau), 28 (William Ervin); Tim Graham Photo Library p. 36.

Cover photograph of an arboreal snake sensing with its tongue reproduced with permission of Getty Images (National Geographic/Tim Laman).

The publishers would like to thank Ann Fullick for her assistance in the preparation of this book.

Every effort has been made to contact copyright holders of any material reproduced in this book. Any omissions will be rectified in subsequent printings if notice is given to the publishers.

Disclaimer
All the Internet addresses (URLs) given in this book were valid at the time of going to press. However, due to the dynamic nature of the Internet, some addresses may have changed or ceased to exist since publication. While the author and publishers regret any inconvenience this may cause readers, no responsibility for any such changes can be accepted by either the author or publishers.

Contents

Some words are shown in bold, **like this**. You can find out what they mean by looking in the glossary.

Introduction to adaptation

An **adaptation** is a change that helps a living thing to survive in its **habitat**. What adaptations make a really successful **predator**? How about a small head, poor eyesight and hearing, or a skinny body and no legs? It does not sound like a successful formula. Yet these are the adaptations of snakes – one of the most successful groups of **vertebrate** predators.

Fangs are the main weapon of many snakes. The fangs of a viper or rattlesnake, such as this pygmy rattlesnake, lie along the roof of the mouth until they are needed.

Reptiles rule!

There are about 2,700 known **species** of snake. Snakes are reptiles – a group that also includes lizards, crocodiles, and turtles. There are about 7,700 reptile species in total.

(Turtles are sometimes called tortoises if they live on land. Throughout this book, the word "turtles" is used for the group that includes both tortoises and turtles.)

WHAT IS A REPTILE?

Reptiles are vertebrates such as crocodiles, lizards, turtles, and snakes. Other vertebrates include mammals, birds, **amphibians**, and fish. Unlike other vertebrates, reptiles have dry scaly skin. Most reptiles lay eggs with shells, although a few species give birth to live young. Reptiles are **cold-blooded**, like amphibians and fish.

From roughly 280 million years ago until 65 million years ago, reptiles were the dominant animals on Earth. **Ichthyosaurs** and **plesiosaurs** swam in the sea, while **pterosaurs** soared through the sky. From about 230 million years ago, dinosaurs were the dominant animals on land. Then, about 65 million years ago, something happened that led to dinosaurs and many other reptiles becoming **extinct**.

Snakes spread

In the history of reptiles, snakes are relative newcomers. The oldest snake fossils are only from about 120 million years ago. The first snakes were lizards that became legless as an adaptation to a burrowing lifestyle. Today, most snakes live above ground. There are snakes all over the world, except Antarctica: in mountains, in forests, in deserts, and in rivers and seas. There are even a few snakes that can glide through the air (see page 9). All snakes have adapted in different ways to their habitats.

Secrets of success

What does it mean to say that snakes are successful? How do we measure their success? Several features of snakes have made them successful. Although they have no legs, their long, thin, flexible bodies means that snakes can glide along the ground fairly quickly. They can also climb, swim, and burrow. Their long, thin bodies are hard to spot, which is good both for sneaking up on **prey** and for hiding from enemies. Even though they are very thin, a snake's extremely flexible jaw and elastic stomach allow it to eat large prey. Many snakes have a **venomous** bite that can paralyse or kill their prey. Snakes that are not venomous kill their prey by squeezing it to death.

The head of this iguana shows the dry scaly skin that covers all reptiles.

How does adaptation work?

Evolution is the process by which life on Earth has developed and changed. Life first appeared on Earth 3.5 billion years ago. Since then, living things have evolved from simple single **cells** to the estimated 10 million or more different species on Earth today.

Male chameleons fight each other for the chance to mate with female chameleons. The best-adapted male will win the fight and mate with the female.

Useful changes

Adaptation is an important part of evolution. Adaptations are ways in which a living thing changes to fit into a particular environment and way of life. For instance, a crocodile's powerful, flattened tail is an adaptation for swimming. A snake's long, thin body was originally an adaptation for burrowing. How, then, does adaptation happen?

Variation

Not all individuals of the same species are exactly the same. You can see this yourself if you look around your class at school. Some people are taller than others; some people have fair hair while others have dark hair. Some people are musical, some are very clever, and some are good at sport. These differences between individuals of a species are known as **variations**.

ALL IN THE GENES

Living things pass on characteristics to their **offspring** through their **genes**. A living thing's genetic material is a kind of "instruction book" for that individual.

Most animals and plants produce offspring by sexual reproduction. Males and females each produce special cells, known as **gametes**, which have only half the normal genetic material. Each parent provides half the genetic information for the offspring.

Natural selection

The variation between individuals is what makes it possible for a species to change and adapt. The driving force for adaptation is called **natural selection**. Different species **compete** with each other for space and for food. Individuals of the same species also compete with each other for the best **mates**. The animals that are best adapted to their environment survive to **reproduce** and pass on their winning characteristics.

If there are changes in the environment where a species lives, natural selection will favour those individuals that have some slight difference that gives them an advantage in the new situation. For example, when the ancestors of snakes first began burrowing, natural selection perhaps favoured thin individuals with shorter legs because they could move faster under ground. Over many generations, thinner animals with short legs were selected, until eventually their bodies became snake-like and their legs were lost altogether.

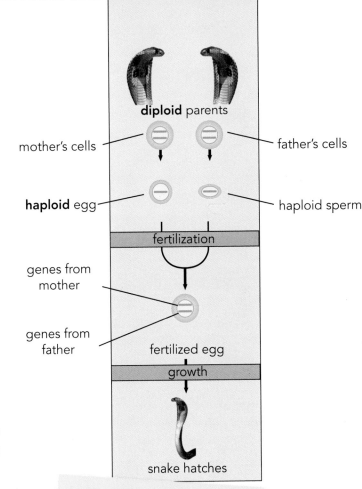

diploid parents

mother's cells — — father's cells

haploid egg — — haploid sperm

fertilization

genes from mother —

genes from father —

fertilized egg

growth

snake hatches

This diagram shows the process of reptile reproduction. Each parent produces gametes (egg cells and sperm cells) that are haploid – they have only half the normal genetic material. When the gametes combine, they form a **fertilized** egg with a full set of genes.

7

Snakes in many habitats

Snakes are legless because their ancestors were burrowers. Some snakes, such as pipe snakes and blind snakes, still spend most of their time under ground. However, most snakes have abandoned burrows and have adapted to living in other habitats.

Sea snakes have adapted to living in water by developing a flattened body which helps them to swim.

Forests, seas, and deserts

Many snakes have adapted to forest life. Snakes that live in trees tend to be thinner and smaller than their cousins that live on the ground. Emerald boas, which live in trees, are much smaller than anacondas, which are ground-living. This adaptation enables the Emerald boas to move easily through the trees. There are also many snakes that live in fresh water or in the sea. Sea snakes have bodies that are flattened side to side, especially at the tail. This flattened shape helps them to swim efficiently.

Snakes have also adapted to life in extreme environments such as deserts. Saving water is the most important thing for survival in the desert, and a snake's scaly skin is very good at keeping in moisture. To avoid the day's heat, desert snakes are most active at night and rest in burrows during the day to keep cool. Several desert snakes move in an unusual looping movement called sidewinding. This is a very efficient way to move over sand.

GLIDING SNAKES

A few forest snakes have evolved a quicker way to get around than climbing. Their bodies are adapted to glide from tree to tree. The paradise flying snake can glide up to 100 metres (328 feet). The snake sucks in its stomach and spreads its ribs out sideways, which makes the snake wider. Then its underside is curved upwards. The whole body is like a long, thin parachute. In the air the snake makes an S-shape, to keep it stable as it glides.

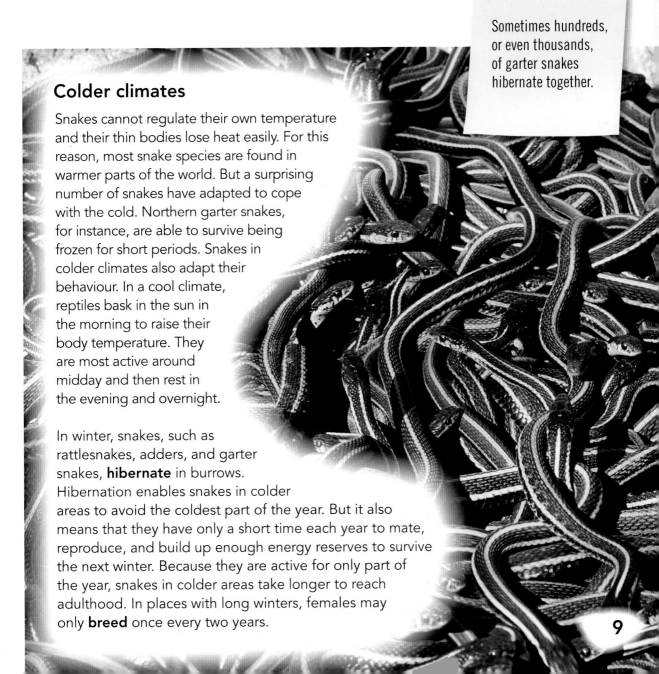

Sometimes hundreds, or even thousands, of garter snakes hibernate together.

Colder climates

Snakes cannot regulate their own temperature and their thin bodies lose heat easily. For this reason, most snake species are found in warmer parts of the world. But a surprising number of snakes have adapted to cope with the cold. Northern garter snakes, for instance, are able to survive being frozen for short periods. Snakes in colder climates also adapt their behaviour. In a cool climate, reptiles bask in the sun in the morning to raise their body temperature. They are most active around midday and then rest in the evening and overnight.

In winter, snakes, such as rattlesnakes, adders, and garter snakes, **hibernate** in burrows. Hibernation enables snakes in colder areas to avoid the coldest part of the year. But it also means that they have only a short time each year to mate, reproduce, and build up enough energy reserves to survive the next winter. Because they are active for only part of the year, snakes in colder areas take longer to reach adulthood. In places with long winters, females may only **breed** once every two years.

Back to the water

Reptiles were the first of the modern vertebrate groups to adapt fully to life on land. Some amphibians, such as frogs, toads, and their relatives, lived on land before reptiles did, but they needed damp conditions to survive and be active. An amphibian's thin skin loses water quickly whereas a reptile's scaly skin is waterproof. Amphibian eggs have a coating of jelly to reduce the risk of them drying out, but this is not as effective as the hard or leathery shell of a reptile's eggs.

Although reptiles are well-adapted to land life, some species have adapted to life in the water. Crocodiles and alligators spend much of their life in water. Many turtle species also live in water – sea turtles hardly ever touch land their whole lives.

With only their eyes and nostrils showing, crocodiles are almost invisible lurking in the water.

Adapting to water

Crocodiles and alligators (crocodilians) are well adapted to **ambush** prey in the water. A crocodilian's flattened tail is adapted to power it through the water. Its eyes and nostrils are right on the top of its head – ideal for lurking just beneath the water's surface with only the eyes and nostrils showing. It can also dive beneath the water and stay there for 15 minutes or longer without breathing.

Crocodilians do not spend all their time in water – they come out on land to sunbathe and warm up their bodies. However, sea turtles do spend their lives in water. Female sea turtles only come ashore to dig a nest and lay their eggs, while male sea turtles never come ashore after leaving their hatching beach. A sea turtle's front and back legs have become flattened into large flippers. The front flippers give most of the swimming power – the turtle flaps its flippers to "fly" through the water. The back flippers trail behind and are used for steering.

There are seven different species of sea turtle. The largest, the leatherback turtle, can survive the cold at depths of over 1,000 metres (3,281 feet) and in oceans far north and south of the Equator. Leatherbacks can keep their core body temperature as much as 18°C (64°F) above the temperature of the water around them. They can do this partly because they have a thick layer of fat beneath their skin, which **insulates** them from the cold. In addition, their blood system is adapted to help them stay warm. Warm blood coming from the core of the body into the flippers warms up cold blood returning from the flippers into the body.

DIGGING IN

Some crocodiles have adapted to life in climates that are too cold or too dry by lying dormant for part of the year. American alligators dig deep "gator holes" in the swamp areas where they live to keep themselves cool in warm weather. In winter they dig burrows where they lie dormant through the cold months. Chinese alligators live in elaborate underground burrows in winter. Australian freshwater crocodiles shelter in burrows when rivers dry up in the dry season.

As cold blood comes back from a turtle's flipper, it meets warm blood coming from the body. The blood coming out warms the blood going back to the body, and so helps the turtle stay warm.

warm blood from body

cold blood coming back from flipper

Swimming in sand; walking on water

There are 4,560 species of lizard – more than any other reptile, including snakes. They have adapted to fit into a wide range of different habitats. On land lizards are more widespread and numerous than any other reptile. However, only a few lizards are good swimmers, while the marine **iguana** is the only species found in the ocean.

Sandfish have a very smooth, polished skin that helps them "swim" through the sand.

Lizards in deserts

Lizards are more at home in deserts than any other animals. Because it is so hot by day, many lizards stay under ground, where it is cooler. They come out to feed in the evening or at night.

One group of geckos that live in the desert have webbed feet. They do not use their feet for swimming but for scooping sand. Another group of lizards known as sandfish "swim" through loose sand by wriggling their bodies.

Agile climbers

Many lizard species are adapted to live in forests. These lizards are generally long-legged and agile – running along branches and jumping between trees. Chameleons are good climbers but they move in slow motion. Their claw-like feet can grip powerfully to branches and they can use their tail as a fifth "leg", wrapping it around a branch for extra stability.

Geckos are another group of excellent climbers. Their feet have large claws or pads covered with millions of tiny hairs that give them a grip, even on glass. The flying dragons of south-east Asia probably have the best way of getting about in the forest. They have large flaps of skin on the sides of their bodies, strengthened by elongated ribs, which open out to form "wings". Flying dragons can glide about 60 metres (200 feet) between trees.

LEGLESS LIZARDS

Snakes are not the only group of legless reptiles. Other lizards have also become specialist burrowers and have lost their legs in the process. Slow worms and snake lizards are just two of several lizard species that look very similar to snakes. Another group of reptiles, the worm-lizards, also look like snakes although they are not snakes, lizards, or worms!

A basilisk lizard is caught in action, running over the water surface.

Walking on water

Although few lizards are regular swimmers, one kind of lizard can walk on water. Basilisk lizards have long toes on their back legs, with flaps of skin along the sides to increase the area of each toe. When it is in danger, the basilisk runs away on its back legs. With its extra-large feet, streams and ponds are no problem – the basilisk just keeps running over the surface of the water.

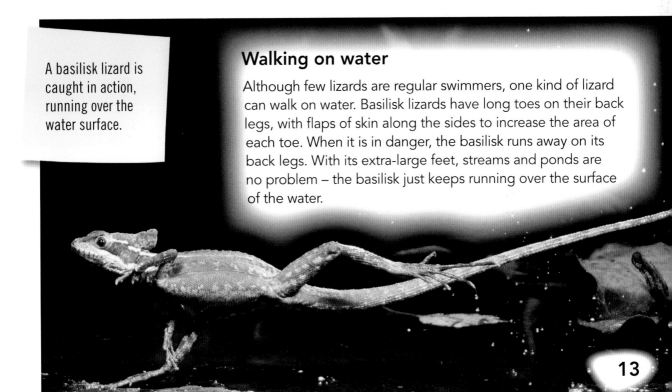

Fanged hunters

All snakes are predators, but they hunt a wide range of different food from insects to mammals as large as deer or even crocodiles. Snakes have many adaptations that help make them successful hunters.

Eyes and ears

Snakes often have poor eyesight and hearing. This is because they lost much of their vision and hearing when they first evolved as burrowing animals. Today, snakes that live on the surface do have eyes, but they are different from those of other animals. Other vertebrates focus by changing the shape of the **lens** in the eye. Snakes, however, focus by moving the lens closer to or further away from the **retina**. This redesigned eye does not work as well as the eyes of other animals.

Snakes have poor hearing for sounds that travel through the air: the sounds that humans hear well. This is because snakes do not have an external ear opening. However, they can hear vibrations through the ground fairly well.

A snake's "nose" is on the roof of its mouth. It is called the Jacobson's organ.

Super senses

To make up for their poor eyesight and hearing, snakes have an excellent sense of smell. Snakes do not have nostrils but instead have smell sensors in two small pits in the roof of the mouth. The snake "tastes" the air with its forked tongue then puts the ends of the tongue into its smell sensors. The sensors pick up any scents caught on the tips of the tongue.

Some snakes, including pit vipers and most boas and pythons, are very sensitive to heat. They have heat sensors on the face that pick up tiny changes in temperature. This helps them to track small mammals and birds by picking up the heat they give off.

No chewing

Snakes have no teeth to chew up their food – they have to swallow it whole. With such a narrow head and body, snakes should be limited to eating small prey. Snakes can open their jaws very wide, however, and the bones of their skull can actually move apart to allow large pieces of food to pass.

Snakes that eat insects, frogs, or other small animals simply swallow them whole and alive. Snakes that attack larger prey need to kill them before they eat them. They use one of two methods. Constrictor snakes wind themselves around their prey and squeeze them until they cannot breathe. Venomous snakes have poison fangs that they sink into their prey. The poison paralyses or kills the prey.

DIFFERENT BODIES

A snake's body shape is adapted to the way it feeds. Snakes such as the gaboon viper are sit-and-wait hunters. They are heavy and thick-bodied because they do not need to move fast. Instead, they need strength when they strike. Snakes such as whip snakes and black racers are fast movers that chase their prey. These snakes have long, thin bodies for getting over the ground quickly.

This egg-eating snake has dislocated its jaw completely. This allows the snake to open its mouth wide enough to swallow the egg.

Other ways of feeding

Reptiles eat many different foods, ranging from underwater plants to buffalos. However, most reptiles are **carnivores**. Crocodiles and alligators are predators of fish and large animals. Many lizards eat insects, although large iguanas eat plants. Most turtles are also predators. However, many turtles eat plants as well as animals, and some species are **herbivorous**.

Crocodiles and alligators

Crocodiles and alligators are fearsome predators. Young crocodiles begin by eating insects and other small prey, but adults eat fish and mammals up to the size of a Cape buffalo, which can weigh 680 kilograms (1,500 pounds). Crocodiles often lurk in waterholes, hidden below the water surface. When animals come to drink, the crocs power themselves out of the water using their tails and grab their victim. Often they drag their prey into the water and hold the animal under water until it drowns.

Lizards

Most lizards are small animals, between 6 and 20 centimetres (2.5 and 8 inches) in length. For lizards this size the main prey are insects. The majority of lizards hunt by day, but geckos are a successful group because they have adapted to hunting at night. A few larger lizard species, such as snake lizards and monitor lizards, eat bigger prey. The largest monitor lizard, the Komodo dragon, often eats deer, pigs, and goats.

Crocodiles can spin themselves in the water with tremendous force. They do this when they have caught a large prey animal to force its head under water. They also do it to tear large pieces off their prey.

DIFFERENT JAWS

Turtles do not have teeth; they have a horny "beak". In sea turtles, this beak is adapted according to their diet. Green and black turtles have saw-tooth beaks, which are good for cutting up the sea grasses they eat. Loggerhead and ridley turtles have heavy, strong beaks for crushing and grinding the crabs and shellfish they feed on. Leatherback turtles eat only soft-bodied jellyfish, so their beak is delicate. Hawksbill turtles have a narrow beak for winkling shrimps and other food out of cracks.

leatherback

loggerhead

The different jaw shapes of different turtle species.

green

hawksbill

Turtles

Most turtles are **omnivores**. Land turtles (tortoises) can only move slowly because of their heavy shells. They therefore feed mainly on insects or slow-moving prey such as slugs and snails.

In the water, many turtles, such as softshell turtles or snapping turtles, are sit-and-wait hunters that eat frogs, worms, fish, and whatever else they can catch. Sea turtles are more active in the water. They can swim as fast as a man can run. Some sea turtles feed on the seabed, but leatherbacks travel long distances hunting for jellyfish.

Unusual feeders

In any habitat, the competition for food and space is fierce. Some animals avoid the competition by finding unusual food sources. Other animals find unusual ways to catch their food that give them the edge over the competition.

Unpopular food

Few animals eat ants and termites. Ants and termites are social insects, and they attack enemies in large groups. However, thread snakes have adapted to actually live in ant or termite nests. Most animals would be attacked if they tried to get into an ant's nest, but thread snakes produce a special scent that calms down the soldier ants guarding the nest. This allows them to live in the nest and snack on the insects whenever they get hungry.

A nasty bite

Komodo dragons are predators, but also **scavengers**. The dead body of a goat or other animal will attract a whole group of these lizards.

When a Komodo dragon is hunting large animals, it usually hides by a well-used animal trail then bursts out, ambushing its victim. The dragon only needs to get in one bite because its mouth is full of harmful bacteria that will quickly infect the wound. With its excellent sense of smell, the Komodo dragon then trails its victim until the injured animal dies. The dragon then devours the body.

A chameleon's tongue is long and has a sticky tip. It can extend its tongue to almost twice the length of its body. The tongue can shoot out to catch an insect in less than a hundredth of a second.

Marine iguanas can dive to depths of around 15 metres (49 feet). They normally dive for only a few minutes, but can survive at least half an hour under water.

Sea vegetarians

Most iguanas are land animals, and several species live in deserts. However, marine iguanas on the Galapagos Islands have evolved the ability to swim and dive. They have webbed feet and their tails are flattened like those of sea snakes and crocodiles, to help with swimming. All these adaptations allow marine iguanas to feed on a very unusual food source for lizards – the seaweed and other **algae** that grow on the seabed. They are the only lizards to feed in the ocean.

The seaweeds that marine iguanas feed on are not very popular foods because they are full of salt. Most animals need salt in their food, but too much salt is dangerous. Marine iguanas therefore have a special **gland** in their nose that gets rid of excess salt.

A TASTE FOR HUMANS

Crocodiles are not fussy eaters – they will attack any animal that comes within their range and is not too big to tackle. As a result, very large crocodiles do sometimes kill and eat people. Nile crocodiles and saltwater crocodiles are the most dangerous species. Nile crocodiles are found in most rivers in Africa, while saltwater crocodiles live along the coasts of India and northern Australia.

19

Snake camouflage

Many animals are **camouflaged** to blend in with their environment. Camouflage works in two ways. It is an important adaptation that helps an animal to avoid predators. Camouflage can hide a snake from enemies such as raccoons and hawks. Camouflage is also important for helping a snake to get close to its prey without being seen.

The patterns on a gaboon viper are very striking against a plain background. But this photo shows how these strong patterns blend in on the forest floor.

Blending or blotchy

Most snakes are coloured to blend in with their background. Desert snakes are sandy coloured, while many tree snakes are green or brown. The eastern brown snake from eastern Australia can be brown, russet, orange, or even black, depending on the habitat it lives in.

Many other snakes have patterns of blotches, diamonds, or stripes along their bodies. These patterns are known as **disruptive camouflage**. The different coloured shapes break up the outline of the snake and make it very difficult to see. The gaboon viper is a large snake with bold brown, cream, and black patterns all over its body. These patterns stand out against a plain background. However, when a gaboon viper is lying coiled among the **leaf litter** in the central African rainforest it is almost invisible. Gaboon vipers are ambush predators – they lie hidden in the leaf litter and wait for prey animals to pass by.

DANGEROUS COLOURS

Snakes, such as coral snakes, have bands of bright colours along their bodies. They stand out against their background rather than blending in. This bright colouring is a warning to predators - coral snakes have **venom** that is deadly even to humans. Animals that try to eat these snakes soon learn that the bright colours are a warning - "keep away, I am poisonous!" The bright colours therefore protect the coral snake from possible predators.

Other, non-poisonous snakes also take advantage of this adaptation. The North American milk snake has almost identical colouring to the poisonous coral snake. Predators avoid the milk snake in the same way that they avoid the coral snake, thinking that this harmless mimic is also poisonous.

By holding itself straight and stiff, the Asian vine snake manages to look like a twig.

Camouflage behaviour

Some snakes are camouflaged by more than colour and patterning. Peringuey's adder is one of several desert snakes that hides itself by digging into the sand until only its eyes and nostrils are visible. Buried in this way it is invisible to both predators and to prey.

The Asian vine snake disguises itself through its behaviour. This thin forest snake lies along the branch of a tree with the front part of the body sticking out from the branch at an angle. In this position it looks remarkably like a twig. The snake completes the illusion by swaying slightly in the breeze. If a prey animal, such as a frog, gets too near to the "twig" it gets a nasty shock!

Camouflage in other reptiles

Most lizards are small animals and they have lots of enemies. Camouflage is an important part of their defence against predators. Turtles also use camouflage – both to hide from predators and to ambush their prey.

Can you see the lizard camouflaged on this rock?

Turtle shells

The colours and patterns of turtles' shells are usually dull and help them to blend in with their environment. Hawksbill turtles and other sea turtles have a darker top to their shell and a light underside. This kind of colouring makes them difficult to spot from above or below. Seen from above, the dark upper shell blends in with the dark background of the ocean depths or the seabed. From below, the light underside blends in with the background of light from the sea's surface. This is called **countershading**.

CROCODILES CAMOUFLAGE

Crocodiles and alligators use the water surface as part of their camouflage. With just their eyes and nostrils above water the rest of their body is just a vague shape when seen from the river bank. They often look like pieces of floating logs. Like sea turtles, crocodilians have light-coloured bellies and dark backs, which make them harder to spot in the water.

Lizard camouflage

Most lizards are coloured to blend in with their environment. Like snakes, many lizards are also speckled or patterned in a way that disrupts their shape and makes them harder to see. Horned lizards, crocodile lizards, and some other species have spines or plates in their skin that make them look like pieces of rock when they are still.

Lizards are generally very active animals. Camouflage colours and patterns are much less effective when an animal is moving. If a lizard feels threatened, and has no hiding place near by, it will freeze and rely on its camouflage to hide it. Lizards can stay still for long periods of time.

Changing colours

Chameleons are especially good at blending in with their surroundings, as they can change colour to fit in with their environment. Combined with their leaf-like shape, this colour-change ability makes chameleons extremely difficult to spot when they are hunting. A few other lizards, such as the Malagasy flat-tailed gecko, can also change their colour.

Chameleons sometimes change colour because of their mood. The oranges and reds in this chameleon's colouring suggest that it is excited or annoyed.

Lizards can change their colour because of special groups of cells in their skin. Each cell in the group contains a different **pigment**. By squeezing its muscles, the lizard can get the cells to change shape. In one shape the colour of the cell is visible, but in another shape the cell's colour does not show. By changing the shapes of the different cells, lizards can change to a variety of different colours.

Leaf tails and head tails

A few reptile species have camouflage adaptations that go beyond colours and patterns. The reptile's whole body is adapted in some way to look like part of the environment.

Leaf-tailed geckos have the ability to make themselves lighter or darker, depending on the colour of their background.

Leaf-like lizards

Many geckos have very good camouflage. Geckos need to find a safe way to rest during the day because they are active at night. One way to do this is to blend in perfectly with their environment.

The body and tail of a leaf-tailed gecko is flattened and shaped to look like a dead leaf. Veins in the skin mimic leaf veins, and the whole tail is twisted to make it look like a curled up leaf. When it lies on a tree branch, fringes around the chin of the leaf-tailed gecko break up the outline of its head. Another mimic, the Sri Lankan kangaroo lizard has legs that look like sticks and a body that looks like a dried leaf.

Other lizard adaptations

The young of the bushveldt lizard protect themselves through mimicry rather than camouflage. Their colour and patterning look like those of the Anthia beetle, which squirts out an acidic spray when attacked. The young lizards also walk in a stiff way, to make their movements resemble that of a beetle.

Turtles in ambush

Another group of animals that rely on camouflage are ambush predators. An ambush predator is one that waits in hiding for its prey. The matamata, a kind of turtle, is an ambush predator that lives in lakes and slow-moving water in the Amazon River basin. It takes camouflage to extremes. The lumps and bumps on the matamata's shell look remarkably like stones. Its flattened, triangular-shaped head is covered with tufts and flaps of flesh, which make it look as if it is covered in weeds. Its superb camouflage can fool even the most wary of fish. When a prey animal comes near enough, the matamata suddenly opens its mouth and the unlucky victim is sucked in.

Some of the skin flaps on the matamata turtle's head can sense movement in the water caused by prey close by.

GRAB MY TAIL!

Skinks are a large group of more than 1,300 lizard species. Most skinks are coloured dull greys and browns to merge in with their habitat, but some species have evolved brightly coloured tails. Like many other lizards, skinks have the ability to shed their tail if an enemy grabs it. Having a brightly coloured tail is an adaptation that draws attention to the tail, distracting any predator from attacking the head and body.

Snake defences

The weapons that a snake uses when attacking prey can also be used to defend against enemies. However, many snakes have other defences that they use when threatened. Whenever possible, a snake will run away or hide from its enemies. Snakes are experts at hiding because they can curl into a tight coil or spread themselves into a long line, which makes it difficult for a predator to know what to look for.

Cobra's heads are small, but the hood makes them look much more threatening.

Looking bigger

If they are cornered many snakes rear up and hiss or growl. Cobras have a flap of skin on either side of their head, which they can open up into a hood. The hood makes the cobra's head and neck look bigger. Hognose snakes also have a cobra-like hood. When threatened these harmless snakes spread their hood, hiss, and strike towards their attacker. South African boomslang snakes inflate their neck area when threatened.

The cottonmouth snake uses another kind of display to startle an attacker. It tips back its head and opens its mouth very wide to show its white lining. Cottonmouths and hognose snakes also produce an unpleasant smell when they are attacked, which puts the predator off.

BALL PYTHONS

Royal pythons are also known as ball pythons. This is because they curl up into a tight ball when they are threatened, with the head hidden in the centre of the ball. This makes it difficult for a predator to attack the python.

Warning rattle

Other snakes make warning noises when under threat. The best known warning sound is the loud, buzzing rattle of a rattlesnake. There are 30 different species of rattlesnake most of which live only in North America. The rattle is produced by specialized dry scales in the tail. Scientists think that the rattle is an adaptation evolved to warn large grazing animals such as bison that the rattlesnake is there. A snake with a rattle is less likely to be trodden on than one without, so it gives rattlesnakes a survival advantage. One group of rattlesnakes live on an island where there are no large grazing animals. These snakes have lost their rattle as it no longer provides an advantage for survival.

Head in the sand

Many snakes do the opposite of cobras when an enemy threatens. They hide their head in the sand or soil and wave their tail. This defence has evolved to encourage predators to strike at the tail rather than the head. In pipe snakes the tail is flattened. When the pipe snake lifts its tail and waves it about it looks like a cobra's head.

This grass snake "plays dead". Grass snakes can stay motionless in this position for 15 minutes or more.

"Playing dead"

Some smaller snakes, such as European grass snakes, "play dead" when attacked by a predator. They lie still, with their mouth open and the tongue hanging out. Snakes that do this sometimes also produce a foul-smelling liquid, which perhaps suggests to predators that they are rotting and unpleasant to eat.

Other reptile defences

Like snakes, other groups of reptiles also have defences against predators. Some of these defences are similar to those of snakes, but some are adaptations that snakes do not use.

Yellow mud turtles belong to the hidden-necked group of turtles, which can withdraw their heads completely into their shells.

Armoured home

Armour is one form of defence that has arisen in other reptile groups, but not among snakes. Turtles have survived for over 200 million years and an important part of their success is their tough shell, which provides portable protection from predators. When attacked, a turtle draws its head and legs into its shell and sits tight. In their armoured casing, turtles are safe from all but very specialized predators.

Turtles can be divided into two groups, depending on how they draw in their heads. Hidden-necked turtles can draw in their heads completely, while side-necked turtles simply fold their head sideways under the front edge of the shell.

More armour

Many crocodilians and lizards are also armoured. Thorny devils and armadillo lizards are armoured with large spikes that make them hard to eat. When an armadillo lizard is threatened it puts its tail in its mouth. This protects the lizards soft belly area, and leaves the predator with a very thorny, awkward mouthful.

All crocodilians have plates of bony armour just under the skin all along their backs. In some species, such as saltwater crocodiles, the bony plates are thin and there is no armour plating on the neck and shoulders. Other crocodilians, such as the black caiman, have thick, tough armour along the back and neck.

Shedding the tail

Another important defence mechanism in lizards is autotomy, (tail-shedding). If a predator grabs their tail, most lizards can shed part of the tail and escape. They can do this because some of the bones in the tail are deliberately weak and break easily. The muscles and blood vessels are also adapted to allow all or part of the tail to be shed quickly.

This green lizard has shed its tail to escape from danger. Although the tail will grow back, it will never be as long, and the new tail cannot be shed.

Spitting, bleeding, and shock tactics

The relationship between a predator and its prey never stands still. Each time a predator evolves new weapons or ways of attacking its prey, the prey animals develop new defences. Some reptiles have developed some amazing defences in response to the threat of predators.

Dangerous spit

If a spitting cobra is threatened it rears up, spreads its hood, and spits venom in the eyes of its enemy. It can hit a predator from more than 3 metres (nearly 10 feet) away. The venom causes temporary blindness and great pain. If a human gets cobra venom in their eye it causes great irritation and, if left untreated, can cause permanent blindness.

Horned lizards from North America do not spit venom, but they can shoot liquid at their attackers. If a horned lizard is grabbed by a predator it squirts blood from special sinuses (blood-filled spaces around its eyes). The blood is foul-tasting and often makes the predator let go.

Spitting cobras "spit" by blowing hard at the same time as letting venom drip from their fangs.

Shock horror

Like snakes, some lizards "play dead" or become very rigid if attacked. This may not seem like much of a defence but many predators have an "attack reflex" that makes them grab prey that move quickly. If the prey stays still, they are less interested.

Other lizards defend themselves by trying to startle their enemies. Again, this may not seem like a very effective defence, but if a lizard can make an attacker pause for just a few seconds it may give the lizard enough time to scurry away to safety.

Frilled lizards startle their enemies by opening their mouth wide and spreading a large "ruff" of skin around the neck. This makes the lizard suddenly look much larger and possibly dangerous, which often makes the predator pause. Blue-tongued skinks from Australia have a very peculiar defence against enemies. They puff up their bodies, hiss, and stick out their bright blue tongues. As with the frilled lizard, the shock can give the skink just enough time to escape.

The Australian-frilled lizard is usually small and harmless looking. However, when it makes its threat display it looks fearsome.

INVISIBLE ENEMIES

One kind of defence in crocodiles and alligators is against invisible enemies – bacteria and other microscopic germs. The water that crocodilians live in is often dirty and full of disease-causing bacteria. Yet the wounds they get in fights and when catching their prey rarely get infected. Scientists have discovered that crocodilians' blood contains a chemical that kills bacteria. This chemical is different from the drugs doctors normally use to fight infections. Scientists may be able to develop a whole new range of useful drugs for humans based on these chemicals.

Snake reproduction

Snakes usually hunt alone and rarely gather in groups with other snakes. However, some species do get together at certain times of year. Male and female snakes also meet up to mate.

Male garter snakes swarm over each other in a frenzy – each one trying to mate with a single female.

Snake meetings

Rattlesnakes and garter snakes often hibernate together. When they emerge from hibernation in spring, garter snakes usually mate immediately. Where large numbers of garter snakes are gathered in one place, many males compete to mate with one female. They form a twisting ball of snakes, with the female at the centre.

Not all snakes hibernate together. Snakes that live alone need a way to find a mate. In most snakes, females that are ready to mate produce a special scent, which they leave behind them wherever they go. Any male that comes across the scent follows the trail to find the female.

Garter snakes are not the only species in which the males compete for females. Mambas, vipers, and rattlesnakes also do this. Two males that want to mate with the same female wrestle with each other. The snakes rear up and twine around each other, each trying to force the other to the ground. The strongest male wins the contest and gets to mate with the female. This means that only the strongest males get to mate.

Eggs versus live young

After mating, many snakes lay eggs. In some species of snake the female produces live young.

Females that lay eggs find a safe place to lay them and then usually leave them to develop on their own. They hide their eggs under logs or rocks, or partly buried in soil, to keep them safe from predators. In colder places, snakes may lay their eggs among rotting plants. The rotting plants produce heat, like a **compost heap** does, and this helps to keep the eggs warm.

All boas and most vipers give birth to live young. Many snakes that live in colder places produce live young. This gives the young snakes a better chance of survival. The eggs are protected inside the female's body until they hatch. She can find the best places to bask and keep the eggs warm. If the weather turns cold she can shelter in a burrow. In snakes that lay eggs, on the other hand, the eggs are at the mercy of the weather.

STORING SPERM

Some female snakes can store sperm inside their bodies after they mate. This allows them to mate at any time, but then wait to produce eggs or young until the weather is good and there is plenty of food available.

Caring for eggs

A few snake species look after their eggs rather than leaving them. Indian pythons pile up their eggs and coil around them. They twitch their muscles to keep their bodies warm, and so warm the eggs. Female king cobras build a pile of leaves and twigs where they lay their eggs. Then they coil up on the eggs and guard them for about 2 months. Once the eggs hatch, the young are left to look after themselves.

After giving birth, female snakes do not care for their young – their offspring are left to fend for themselves.

Reproduction in turtles and lizards

Like snakes, most turtles and lizards live alone rather than in groups. Among lizards, it is usually the male who courts the female, but in turtles the females are involved in courtship. All turtles and most lizards lay eggs, but a few lizards also produce live young.

Some male lizards use displays to compete for females, but these blue-tongued skinks are fighting for the chance to mate.

Turtle courtship

Before a male turtle can mate, he often has to fight off rivals for a female. Fights between turtles can be serious, with rivals often wounding each other quite badly. Once a male has beaten off any rivals, there is often a long courtship ritual with the female before mating. Wood turtles do a courtship dance together in which they walk towards each other and swing their heads from side to side. This dance may go on for several hours.

Colourful lizards

In some cases male lizards may fight to attract females. Some male chameleons have horns, which they use to grapple with each other. Other lizards put on visual displays. Male anoles have an area of brightly coloured skin on their throat, which they can blow up to make a colourful display to attract a female.

It might seem that colourful courtship displays would decrease survival chances for male lizards. Snakes catch more male anoles than females, probably because of their display behaviour. However, it is no good for a male to survive if he cannot reproduce.

Eggs and young

Most turtles lay their eggs in a flask-shaped nest dug in the soil or sand. Often turtles make an effort to disguise the nest site. River terrapins dig a false nest at a distance from the real one, or sometimes divide the eggs between several nests. With a number of separate nest sites predators may find one nest but miss others.

Some lizards lay eggs, while others give birth to live young. As with snakes, lizards that produce live young often live in colder regions. Most egg-laying lizards produce eggs with leathery shells, which are not waterproof. However, most geckos produce hard-shelled eggs that are waterproof.

TRAVELLING TURTLES

Sea turtles begin their lives on beaches then travel long distances over many years, following ocean currents or sources of food. When the turtles become adults they go back to mate in the ocean near the beaches where they were born. They do this because the eggs need to be laid on land and the turtles' home beaches are good nesting sites. Green turtles may **migrate** 4,500 kilometres (2,800 miles) to reach their nesting sites. After mating, the females go ashore to lay their eggs.

Young olive ridley sea turtles emerging from their nest. Many will be killed by predators on the short trip from the nest to the sea.

Good parents

Unlike most other reptiles, crocodiles and alligators live in loosely organized social groups. Crocodilians all lay eggs, but they take more care of them than other reptiles.

Group living

Crocodilians often gather together in groups to bask in the sun or to cool down at a waterhole. In these groups, crocodiles use visual signals and noises to sort out a pecking order – that is, which crocodiles are dominant. Once this has been established, the crocodiles generally ignore each other and there are few fights.

For most crocodilians there are definite advantages to getting along in groups. Good nesting sites, basking sites, or waterholes are often limited, and without some sort of social structure crocodiles would have to fight every time they wanted to bask in the sun or cool off in the water. Co-operation can also be useful when feeding. Nile crocodiles gather each year at Lake St Lucia in southern Africa to catch mullet; a kind of fish.

Once a group of crocodiles have established a "pecking order", they can rest or bask close together without conflict.

Guarding the eggs

Like turtles, crocodilians are egg layers. Different species lay between 20 and 80 eggs. Some dig holes in the ground for their eggs, while others build nests of plant material. As the plants rot they heat up, like a **compost heap**, which keeps the eggs warm. Female crocodiles guard their nests, and when the eggs are ready to hatch they break them open so that the young can get out. Without this care and attention many more eggs would fall victim to egg-stealers, such as snakes and monitor lizards.

Some crocodilians, such as the saltwater crocodile and the Nile crocodile, carry on protecting their offspring after they have hatched. Once the eggs have hatched, the female gathers all the young hatchlings up in her mouth and carries them to a sheltered, shallow "nursery pool". Here she guards the young crocs for several weeks. This gives the young a chance to learn to feed and to grow before they are left unprotected.

SEX AND TEMPERATURE

The temperature at which crocodilian eggs **incubate** is extremely important, because it affects whether the hatchlings are male or female! In saltwater crocodiles, eggs that incubate at around 32°C (90°F) hatch out as males, while eggs that are hotter or cooler than this hatch as females. Scientists are still working to understand how this dependence on temperature has evolved and what benefit it could have for the crocs.

A newly hatched Nile crocodile emerges from its shell.

Food, medicines, and skins

Reptiles have survived natural changes and disasters for over 230 million years. However, human activities threaten the existence of all kinds of reptile. Turtles and crocodiles are in particular danger because they grow slowly and produce relatively few offspring. If the population of a species drops it takes years for the numbers to recover.

Turtles on sale at a market in Guangzhou, China. All turtle species are hunted for food and for use in traditional Chinese medicines.

Hunted for skins and shells

Over-hunting is a particular problem for crocodilians and turtles. Crocodiles and alligators have been hunted for many years for their skins. Those species with less armour, such as saltwater crocodiles, are especially at risk because their skins produce better leather. Many crocodilians are also killed because they are seen as a danger to humans.

Many turtle species are heavily hunted for various reasons. Sea turtles have suffered particularly badly. In the past, hawksbill turtles were intensely hunted for their beautiful shells, while olive ridley turtles were killed in huge numbers for their leather. Green turtles have been hunted for their meat and eggs, and for the green fat on their bodies that is used to make turtle soup. Today these turtles are often hunted illegally, and their eggs are collected illegally at breeding times.

All turtle species of China and south-east Asia have been heavily hunted for food and for making traditional medicines. More recently, many wild turtles have been captured each year to be sold as pets. The turtles are often transported in very poor conditions and many of them die during the journey.

Crocodiles are now widely farmed for their skins and meat. Initially, wild eggs were collected and raised to become adults, but now the crocs are bred in captivity.

A crocodile success story

In the 1970s, saltwater crocodiles in northern Australia were close to extinction. The crocodiles were so heavily hunted that numbers had fallen by 95 percent. Very few adults were left in the wild.

Through the work of conservationists, saltwater crocodiles were brought back from extinction within about 20 years. At first, wild saltwater crocodiles were strictly protected and farms were set up to raise crocodiles for skins and meat. Today there are around 75,000 wild saltwater crocodiles in northern Australia.

SAVING ASIA'S TURTLES

Most species of turtle in Asia are now in danger of becoming extinct because so many are being killed for food and for making medicines. Some turtles have been listed as protected species, and some protected areas have been set up in China and southeast Asia. However, turtles continue to disappear at an alarming rate. The best hope for saving wild turtles may be to set up turtle farms where animals can be bred for meat, eggs, and medicines.

Disappearing habitats

Although over-hunting is of great concern, the loss of habitats is the greatest risk to the world's reptiles. As the human population grows, more and more of the world's natural environment is being destroyed. Forests are cut down for wood and to make space for farmland and buildings. Swamps are drained and grasslands become farmland. Reptiles that cannot adapt to these changing habitats cannot survive.

On the edge of extinction

Chinese alligators live at the mouth of the Yangtze River in China, in wetland habitats. Chinese alligators are smaller than their closest relations, the American alligators. They measure a maximum of 2 metres (6 feet 6 inches) in length. Chinese alligators feed at night, mainly on snails, mussels, and other shellfish.

There are very few Chinese alligators left in the wild – probably less than 200 individuals. The main reason for their disappearance is the loss of their habitat. The alligators are found only in small areas of swampy land surrounded by farmland. The different groups of wild alligators are not in contact, and unless some habitat is recovered these alligators will probably die out.

Over 10,000 Chinese alligators have been bred in captivity and a few of these are now being released into the wild.

Alien intruders

Another major threat to reptiles is the introduction of new animals into their habitat. Animals such as rats, rabbits, dogs, and cats have been introduced by humans to many areas. This can have a huge effect on local reptiles.

New Zealand is the only place in the world where you can find tuataras – two rare species of reptile that are closely related to lizards. On the New Zealand mainland tuataras have been wiped out completely by the introduction of mammals such as cats and rats. Cats hunted and killed the tuataras, while rats competed with them for food and living space. Tuataras now survive only on 30 small islands where there are no cats or rats.

GALAPAGOS INVASION

Another species that is under threat from alien invaders is the world's biggest land turtle, the Galapagos giant turtle. These huge animals can grow to 1.2 metres (4 feet) in length and can weigh up to 320 kilograms (about 700 pounds). Galapagos turtles are grazing animals that eat grasses and other plants. They are in danger of becoming extinct because many of the plants they normally graze on are being eaten by goats, which were originally brought to the island by humans and have now run wild. On the island of Pinta, only one giant turtle has survived the goat invasion. This turtle and many others are now part of a captive breeding programme to try and rescue the Galapagos turtles.

A Galapagos giant turtle at the Charles Darwin Research Station, part of the Charles Darwin Foundation. Scientists here conduct research and environmental education for Galapagos conservation.

Already extinct

In the 230 million years since reptiles first appeared on Earth, many species and larger groups of reptiles have become extinct. Some of these reptiles died out because of direct competition from other, better adapted species. More often, species and whole groups of reptiles died out because the environment changed and they were unable to adapt to the changed conditions.

The dinosaur extinction

Probably the largest extinction of reptiles happened 65 million years ago, when dinosaurs became extinct. Other large groups of reptiles also died out at this time, including pterosaurs (reptile "birds") and large sea reptiles known as mosasaurs. There is huge debate over why this great extinction happened, but the most likely cause is thought to be a giant **meteorite** from space, which hit the Earth on the Yucatán Peninsula of Mexico. Clouds of dust and smoke from the **meteorite** crash affected the climate worldwide and had disastrous effects on all life.

Most of the species that died out in the dinosaur extinction were large animals. Many more small species, such as the mammals that existed at the time, survived. This may be simply because small animals could survive on much less food.

More big animals

Much more recently, between 1.8 million and 10,000 years ago, another group of large animals roamed the Earth. These included many large mammals, such as mammoths and sabre-tooth cats, and giant birds called teratorns with a wingspan of 7.5 metres (25 feet). There were also some huge reptiles. These included a giant lizard, Megalania, over 7 metres (23 feet) long, and a giant snake, Gigantophis, that could have been around 10.7 metres (35 feet) long and perhaps ate the ancestors of modern elephants.

All these giant animals died out between 100,000 and 10,000 years ago. Over much of this time the Earth was in the grip of an ice age, when many parts of northern Europe and North American were covered by huge ice sheets. This global cooling may have been the cause of these extinctions, although many of the species had survived earlier ice ages.

Modern extinctions

Some scientists think that over-hunting by prehistoric humans was the cause of the giant animal extinction, although many other scientists disagree. Today, however, most scientists agree that human activities are threatening to cause the extinction of many more reptile species. Only serious conservation efforts can save some of these reptiles.

Mosasaurs are the ancestors of modern monitor lizards. It was believed that they might also be the ancestors of modern snakes, but this idea is now thought to be unlikely.

Further information

Reptile records

Biggest reptile	saltwater crocodile	Largest grow to over 7 m (22 ft.)
Longest reptile	reticulated python	Longest measured 11.4 m (37 ft. 6 in.)
Most poisonous snake	beaked sea snake	One drop of venom is strong enough to kill three 70 kg (154 lb.) people. However, the sea snake has a small amount of venom and rarely bites.
Most deadly bite	king cobra	Venom is 100 times weaker than that of sea snake. However, it has enough venom to kill an African elephant with one bite.
Longest-lived reptile	Galapagos giant turtle	One turtle is known to have lived 175 years
Deepest diver	leatherback turtle	Can dive to depths of 1,200 m (3,940 ft.)
Biggest ever reptile	seismosaurus (plant-eating dinosaur)	About 39–52 m (130–170 ft.) long. It lived 156 to 145 million years ago.
Biggest ever marine reptile	liopleurodon (type of plesiosaur)	Up to 15 m (49 ft.) long. It lived 165 to 150 million years ago.

Reptile classification

Reptiles can be divided into three main groups: turtles and tortoises, lizards and snakes, and crocodiles and alligators. The lizards and snakes are by far the largest group. There is also a separate group containing just two species of tuatara (lizard-like animals) found only in New Zealand.

Group	Number of species	Facts and figures
Turtles and tortoises		
Turtles and tortoises	293	Smallest turtle: flattened musk turtle and bog turtle – 11 cm (4 in.) Largest turtle: leatherback – up to 244 cm (96 in.)

Lizards and snakes		
Lizards	4,560	Smallest lizard: Jaragua gecko – 1.5 cm (0.6 in.) Largest lizard: Komodo dragon – 150 cm (59 in.)
Worm-lizards	140	Sizes from 10 to 75 cm (4 to 30 in.)
Crocodiles and alligators		
Crocodiles and alligators	23	Smallest crocodile: dwarf caiman – 1.2 m (4 ft.) Largest crocodile: saltwater crocodile – 7 m (22 ft.)
Tuataras		
Tuataras	2	Size from 45 to 61 cm (18 to 24 in.)

Books

- Ernst, Carl. H. & Zug, George. R. *Snakes in Question* (Smithsonian Institution, 1996)
  – The answers to frequently asked questions about snakes, written by two world experts

- Solway, Andrew. *Wild Predators: Deadly Reptiles* (Heinemann Library, 2005)
  – Learn about the different deadly ways that reptiles hunt their prey

- Solway, Andrew. *Wild Predators: Deadly Snakes* (Heinemann Library, 2005)
  – Learn about the different ways these fanged hunters overcome their victims

- Spilsbury, Louise & Richard. *Animals Under Threat: Alligator*
    (Heinemann Library, 2004)
  – Highlights the threat facing these endangered animals

Websites

- Charles Darwin Foundation
  www.darwin foundation.org
  – Information about the Foundation's Galapagos conservation and research work

- Queensland Museum
  www.qmuseum.qld.gov.au/features/snakes/
  – Australia has more venomous snakes than anywhere else in the world. Learn about
    120 of them on this website.

- The Rudiments of Wisdom Encyclopedia
  www.rudimentsofwisdom.com/themes/themes_animals.htm
  – This cartoon encyclopedia has fun articles on turtles, crocodiles,
    and dinosaurs.

Glossary

adaptation change that helps a living thing fit into its environment

algae tiny plant-like living things. Seaweeds are an example of algae.

ambush make a surprise attack from hiding

amphibian animal with smooth skin that lays eggs in a jelly-coating and usually spends part of its life in water and part on land

breed mate and produce young

camouflage colours and patterns that help an animal blend in with its environment

carnivore animal that eats meat

cell tiny building block of all living things

chromosome tiny thread-like structure found in the nuclei of most living cells, carrying genetic information in the form of genes

cold-blooded an animal is cold-blooded if it cannot keep its body temperature constant and relies on the environment to heat or cool it

compete try and win

compost heap pile of garden and kitchen refuse that decomposes to produce compost

countershading colouring that makes an animal's body look flat and less obvious

diploid (of a cell or a nucleus) containing two complete sets of chromosomes, one from each parent

disruptive camouflage markings that break up an animal's outline and make it harder to see

evolution gradual changes over time in a group of living things

extinct no longer in existence

fertilization cause an egg, female animal, or plant to develop a new individual by introducing male reproductive material

gamete male and female sex cell – usually sperm and eggs

gene thing that is transferred from a parent to its offspring that determines some characteristics of that offspring

gland part of the body that produces some kind of liquid

habitat place where an animal lives

haploid (of a cell or a nucleus) having a single set of chromosomes

herbivore animal that feeds on plants

hibernate sleep through the winter

ichthyosaur giant ocean reptile that looked similar to a dolphin and lived from 250 million years ago until about 90 million years ago

iguana group of about 700 lizard species found mostly in North and South America

incubate keep eggs warm so that they can develop and hatch

insulate protect from heat or cold

leaf litter layer of dead and rotting leaves on the floor of a forest

lens part of the eye behind the iris that focuses light on to the retina

mate animal's breeding partner; also when a male and female animal come together to produce young

meteorite rock that falls from space and hits Earth's surface

migrate travel long distances each year from a summer breeding area to a winter feeding ground

natural selection mechanism of evolution by which only those individuals that are best fitted to their habitat and lifestyle survive and reproduce

offspring young of an animal

omnivore animal that eats both animal and plant food

pigment natural colour of a plant or animal

plesiosaur large ocean reptile with a long neck and paddle-like limbs that lived from 220 to 65 million years ago

predator animal that hunts and eats other animals

prey animal that is eaten by a predator

pterosaur first vertebrate to fly. Lived from 228 to 65 million years ago.

reproduce produce offspring

retina light-sensitive layer inside the eye

scavenger animal that feeds on dead and rotting animals or other kinds of waste

species group of animals that are similar and can breed together to produce healthy offspring

variation differences between individuals within a species

venom poison

venomous poisonous

vertebrate animal with a backbone

Index